IRWIN

Q
QUICK START MASTERS

TECHNOLOGY

TECHNOLOGY
LEVEL A
Grades 1–2

Project Coordinator and Contributor: Ruth Brandon

Contributors: Lydia Cartlidge, Gary Gibson,
Marilyn L. Legault, Claudette Sims, Elizabeth Verrall

Reproducible Activities
Using Classroom Technology

Cover and title page art: Paul Wiersma
Cover Design: Donna Guilfoyle/ArtPlus Limited
Interior Design: ArtPlus Limited
Page Makeup: Leanne Knox/ArtPlus Limited
Edited by: Jeff Siamon

1 2 3 4 5 01 00 99 98 97 96
Printed in Canada

Published by
Irwin Publishing
1800 Steeles Avenue West
Concord, ON L4K 2P3

Contents

Introduction

Looking at Technology

Technology, part of Irwin Publishing's elementary reproducible activity masters series *Quick Starts*, is a series of activity-based books that bring technology into the classroom. Use them with your students as stand-alone lessons or as a starting point from which to integrate the use of technology with curriculum. These activities have been designed by teachers (and classroom tested!) to provide problem-solving approaches to common themes and subject areas. Here students will find a variety of interesting and self-motivating things to do that can accommodate their various learning styles and developmental stages. Many activities are in an open format.

But *Technology* is not a study course in technology in itself. Rather, it challenges students to use technology as a *tool* in achieving their learning objectives. This distinction is important. Just as mathematics can be studied as a subject in itself, so it also can be employed to solve problems in other subject areas. Similarly, technology in the classroom is able to extend students' problem-solving abilities. In an increasingly complex and changing world, students must acquire the knowledge, skills, and strategies that will help them function. Understanding and using technology is an important part of this acquisition.

You might want, however, to explore with your students the broader concept of technology (if you haven't already done so). Certainly, it can be a much misunderstood term—not just electronics and computers. The ancient Egyptians employed technology to build the pyramids long before the first microchip. So while students will use many "state-of-the-art" devices, they will also utilize ordinary cameras, overhead projectors, common tools (probably the oldest form of technology), and other mechanical and electrical apparatuses.

Looking at Contents

Each book in the *Technology* series includes twenty-eight theme-based activities in one of the following curriculum areas:
- Social Studies and Fine Art,
- Science and Technology,
- Language Arts,
- Mathematics.

There are three achievement levels and books for each of the above subjects:
- Level A—Grades 1 and 2,
- Level B—Grades 3 and 4,
- Level C—Grades 5 and 6.

Of course, these levels can be adapted to suit the learning abilities of your students.

A teacher resource page is on the back of each reproducible student activity sheet. Each activity is identified by a Title, Theme, and Subject, as well as by a graphic that represents the theme. (The same graphic is on both the teacher and student pages.) Also identified on the teacher resource page are the activity's Materials list, Learning Outcomes, Inquiry/Thinking Skills, and Learning Strategies. The latter information might be especially useful when creating tracking and evaluation forms.

Icons on the bottom of each activity sheet indicate which technologies will be used. (See inside front cover for a complete list.) As well, suggestions for activity groupings are shown.

Three matrixes have been included for your convenience:
- theme and technology matrixes for this book;
- subject theme matrix for all the books in this curriculum area.

Looking at Science and Technology, Levels A, B, and C

The Science and Technology books in the *Technology* series cover such topics as:

- life science,
- earth and space science,
- physical science,
- the study of nature and the environment.

These activities will provide students with some of the skills and information about the natural world they will need in order to prepare them for an increasingly scientific and technological society.

Using these activities, students will develop the ability to employ a wide variety of methods and practices to solve problems. Younger students will use these activities to learn about technology through play. Older students will follow basic scientific methods and technology design processes. Inherent in these processes is the need for creative problem solving and risk taking. The real-life applications in these activities will help students relate the hypotheses they have discovered to other areas of learning, as well as to their daily lives.

Theme Matrix
Science and Technology, Level A

Theme	Title	Groupings*	Technology
Bears	28/Winter Dens	•• Pairs, Groups, Class	(icons)
Colour	14/Making Colours	• Individual, Class	(icons)
	17/Mixing Colours	• Individual, Pairs	(icons)
Communication	13/Looking at the Computer Keyboard	Pairs, Class	(icon)
	25/Telephone of the Future	Pairs, Class	(icons)
Earth	12/Looking at Sand	Pairs, Groups, Class	(icons)
Environment	5/Fall Colours	Individual, Pairs, Class	(icons)
	11/Living and Non-living Things	Individual, Pairs, Class	(icon)
	20/Reduce, Reuse, and Recycle Paper	Groups, Class	(icon)
	26/Weather Watch—1	Pairs, Groups, Class	(icons)
	27/Weather Watch—2	Pairs, Groups, Class	(icons)
Experiments	2/Bubble Blowing	Groups, Class	(icon)
	7/Fun with Mirrors	Individual, Pairs, Class	(icon)
	15/Making Sound	Groups, Class	(icon)
	18/Oral Observations	Groups	(icons)
	22/Sound Travel	Pairs, Groups	(icons)
Family	24/Technology in Our House	Individual, Pairs, Groups, Class	(icons)
Food	1/Apples and Other Fruits	Individual, Groups, Class	(icons)
Light	21/Shadow Fun	Individual, Groups	(icons)
Machines	8/Gears That Make Patterns	Individual, Pairs, Class	(icons)
	9/Lever Beaver	Individual, Class	(icons)
	10/Levers in the Classroom	Groups, Class	(icons)
	16/Media Gadgets	Groups, Class	(icons)
	19/Pulley Magic!	Pairs, Groups, Class	(icons)
Plants	23/Sprouting Ideas	Individual, Groups	(icons)
Time	4/Changes over Time	Groups, Class	(icon)
Transportation	3/Building Bridges	Individual, Groups	(icons)
	6/Four Wheels to Go	Pairs, Groups, Class	(icons)

* Groupings: • = Individual; •• = Pairs; ⦂ = Groups; ⦂⦂ = Class

Technology Matrix
Science and Technology, Level A

Technology	Title	Theme	Groupings*
cassette tape	18/Oral Observations	Experiments	Groups
	26/Weather Watch—1	Environment	Pairs, Groups, Class
	27/Weather Watch—2	Environment	Pairs, Groups, Class
books	9/Lever Beaver	Machines	Individual, Class
	16/Media Gadgets	Machines	Groups, Class
	24/Technology in Our House	Family	Individual, Pairs, Groups, Class
	26/Weather Watch—1	Environment	Pairs, Groups, Class
	27/Weather Watch—2	Environment	Pairs, Groups, Class
paintbrush & pencil	3/Building Bridges	Transportation	Individual, Groups
	5/Fall Colours	Environment	Individual, Pairs, Class
	6/Four Wheels to Go	Transportation	Pairs, Groups
	9/Lever Beaver	Machines	Individual, Class
	12/Looking at Sand	Earth	Pairs, Groups
	25/Telephone of the Future	Communications	Pairs
	28/Winter Dens	Bears	Pairs, Groups, Class
building bricks	3/Building Bridges	Transportation	Individual, Groups
	6/Four Wheels to Go	Transportation	Pairs, Groups, Class
	8/Gears That Make Patterns	Machines	Individual, Pairs, Class
	9/Lever Beaver	Machines	Individual, Class
	19/Pulley Magic!	Machines	Pairs, Groups
	25/Telephone of the Future	Communications	Pairs, Class
camera	21/Shadow Fun	Light	Individual, Groups
CD	3/Building Bridges	Transportation	Individual, Groups
	5/Fall Colours	Environment	Individual, Pairs, Class
	9/Lever Beaver	Machines	Individual, Class
	19/Pulley Magic!	Machines	Pairs, Groups, Class
	22/Sound Travel	Experiments	Pairs, Groups
	28/Winter Dens	Bears	Pairs, Groups, Class
hourglass	12/Looking at Sand	Earth	Pairs, Groups, Class
laptop	11/Living and Non-living Things	Environment	Individual, Pairs, Class
	13/Looking at the Computer Keyboard	Communication	Pairs, Class
	23/Sprouting Ideas	Plants	Individual, Groups, Class

*Groupings: • = Individual; •• = Pairs; ⁞ = Groups; ⁚⁚ = Class

Technology Matrix
Science and Technology, Level A

Technology	Title	Theme	Individual	Pairs	Groups	Class
	24/Technology in Our House	Family	•	••	✓	✓
	26/Weather Watch—1	Environment		••	✓	✓
	2/Bubble Blowing	Experiments			✓	✓
	20/Reduce, Reuse, and Recycle Paper	Environment			✓	✓
	7/Fun with Mirrors	Experiments	•	••		✓
	14/Making Colours	Colour	•			✓
	16/Media Gadgets	Machines			✓	✓
	10/Levers in the Classroom	Machines			✓	✓
	18/Oral Observations	Experiments			✓	
	23/Sprouting Ideas	Plants	•			✓
	25/Telephone of the Future	Communications		••		✓
	27/Weather Watch—2	Environment		••	✓	
	1/Apples and Other Fruits	Food	•		✓	✓
	10/Levers in the Classroom	Machines			✓	✓
	14/Making Colours	Colour	•			✓
	17/Mixing Colours	Colours	•	••		
	1/Apples and Other Fruits	Food	•		✓	✓
	21/Shadow Fun	Light	•		✓	
	6/Four Wheels to Go	Transportation		••	✓	✓
	8/Gears That Make Patterns	Machines	•	••		✓
	10/Levers in the Classroom	Machines			✓	✓
	15/Making Sound	Experiments			✓	✓
	16/Media Gadgets	Machines			✓	✓
	19/Pulley Magic!	Machines		••	✓	✓
	22/Sound Travel	Experiments		••	✓	
	25/Telephone of the Future	Communications		••		✓
	4/Changes over Time	Time			✓	✓
	1/Apples and Other Fruits	Food	•		✓	✓
	26/Weather Watch—1	Environment		••	✓	✓
	27/Weather Watch—2	Environment		••	✓	✓

*Groupings: • = Individual; •• = Pairs; ⦙ = Groups; ⦂⦂ = Class

Apples and Other Fruit

Name _____

1. Apple words:

_____   _____   _____
_____   _____   _____
_____   _____   _____

2. Draw the fruit you like to eat.

Title:	**Apples and Other Fruit**
Theme:	**Food**
Subject:	**Science and Technology**

Materials Needed: Various kinds of apples, seeds from an assortment of fruit, samples and photographs of various fruits, overhead projector, acetates and marking pens, magnifying glasses, sorting hoops, blank flash cards.

Learning Outcomes:
• Compare and contrast basic characteristics of living things.
• Ask questions about the world around them and look for answers to these questions, working both alone and with others.
• Participate actively in math, science, and technology activities.

Inquiry/Thinking Skills: Analysis, application, comprehension, knowledge, and synthesis.

Learning Strategies: Brainstorming, observing, recording, researching, sorting, and viewing for information.

TEACHING STRATEGIES

1. Have students view a filmstrip or videotape about apples. Discuss the different kinds of apples and show them some samples. Identify the apple names. Have students observe with magnifying glasses the skin of the various apples. Help them create a word list on their activity sheets to describe their appearance.

2. Ask students to do a taste test of the apple samples and record words to describe the flavour and consistency (crisp, soft, hard, sour, tart, sweet, mushy, etc.). They can add these to their activity sheets. Complete a class tally chart of the students' favourite apples.

3. Next, have students cut an apple in half and observe its core and seeds using a magnifying glass. Ask them: "Do seeds from different apples look the same?" Discuss why apples have seeds and how apples grow.

4. Pose the question: "What other foods have seeds?" Brainstorm a list of fruit, showing sample pictures. Have students write the names of these fruits on cards. Encourage them to draw the fruit(s) they like to eat on their activity sheets.

5. Divide students into small groups to sort the fruit cards using sorting hoops. Groups of students can record their results on an overhead projector.

Bubble Blowing

Name _____

1. Find a better bubble blower.

How We Blew Bubbles	Very Good	Good	Not Good
Electric Hair Blower			
Electric Fan			
Electric Mixer			
Hand Mixer (egg beater)			
Bellows			
Cardboard Fan			
Straw			
Whisk			
Other			
Other			

Title:	**Bubble Blowing**
Theme:	**Experiments**
Subject:	**Science and Technology**

Materials Needed: Commercial bubble juice or "homemade" mixture (3 parts water to 1 part dish-washing detergent [Joy] and 1 part glycerin), plastic, cotton pipe cleaners or wire wand, bowl for bubble juice, electric hair blower, fan, bellows and mixer, hand mixer, whisk, cardboard sheet, chart paper, markers, straw.

Learning Outcomes:
- Identify everyday examples.
- Investigate devices that make use of the properties of various forms of energy.
- Investigate and describe simple cause-and-effect relationships related to bubble blowing.

Inquiry/Thinking Skills: Analysis, application, comprehension, evaluation, and synthesis.

Learning Strategies: Comparing, demonstrating, rating, and substituting.

TEACHING STRATEGIES

1. Allow students some time to experiment with bubble blowing using the bubble juice and the wand. Brainstorm with the students other kinds of energy devices which could also perform the same function of blowing and dispersing bubbles. Create a list on chart paper.

2. Direct students to work in groups to test which device can blow soap bubbles the best. Set up centres or stations for each device listed on their activity sheets.

3. Place the wand into the bowl of soapy water. Hold up the wand and let the electric hair blower force the air through the wand. Ask: "Does it create a good bubble?" Have students record their results on their activity sheets by putting a check mark in the correct column. Try the experiment at least three times before asking them to make a final decision.

4. Have each group go to the next station and repeat the experiment using the device at this station.

5. Ask students: "Which one was the best bubble blower? Why? Which one was the second best? Why? Which one was the worst? Why?"

6. Challenge them to sort their bubble makers from best to worst.

Building Bridges

Name _____

1. Look at different bridges in a CD-ROM encyclopedia.
   Draw one of these bridges.

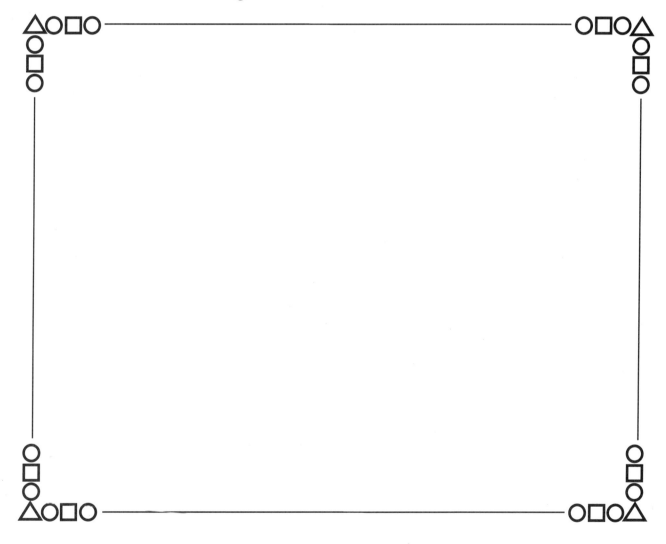

2. Build the strongest bridge you can. Use the materials your teacher
   gives you.

3. Test how strong your bridge is.

Title:	**Building Bridges**
Theme:	**Transportation**
Subject:	**Science and Technology**

Materials Needed: Straws, tubes, spaghetti, glue, tape, fasteners, etc. (materials to build bridges), CD-ROM encyclopedia for research on bridges.

Learning Outcomes:
• Demonstrate knowledge of how to build a structure.
• Work constructively with others on projects.

Inquiry/Thinking Skills: Evaluation and synthesis.

Learning Strategies: Building, creating, and observing.

TEACHING STRATEGIES

1. Let students observe different shapes of bridges in a CD-ROM encyclopedia (suspension, arch, cantilever, truss, etc.). Challenge students to draw one of these bridges.

2. Invite students to build the strongest bridge possible. Bridges will be tested to determine which can support the most weight.

3. Explain what a "fair test" is: *Everyone must have the same quantity and type of material and the same span of bridge.* Students can use spaghetti and white glue, cardboard tubes and fasteners, straws and tape or whatever materials are easily available.

4. Tell them to build their bridges, and then test them by applying weights.

SOMETHING TO THINK ABOUT

▶ Encourage students to try building structures with various geometric shapes (round, triangular, square, etc.). Ask them: "What shapes seem to be the strongest?"

▶ Crack four empty eggs in half. Place the four half eggs on a solid surface in a square, cut side down. Test the strength of the eggs by carefully placing a book on them. Estimate how many books the eggs will support before breaking. Discuss why eggs are so strong.

Changes over Time

Name _____

1. Three ways I have changed:
   a) _____
   b) _____
   c) _____

2. Changes in other things:
   a) _____
   b) _____
   c) _____

3. Show what changes you think will happen.

Title Frame	Before
During	After

Title:	**Changes over Time**
Theme:	**Time**
Subject:	**Science and Technology**

Materials Needed: Video camera.

Learning Outcomes:
• Record some changes in themselves, other people, and the world around them.
• Produce a simple message with a video camera.

Inquiry/Thinking Skills: Application, comprehension, and synthesis.

Learning Strategies: Operating, organizing, and sequencing.

TEACHING STRATEGIES

1. Through the use of videos, photographs, stories, and computer programs, encourage students to observe the changes that happen in the world around them.

2. List the changes the students have observed. These changes might include:

- shadows
- burning birthday candle
- the seasons
- growth of plants, animals, people
- melting snowballs
- weather
- effects of wear and use on objects

3. Demonstrate to students the use and care of the video camera. Have them work in groups of four so that each person has a chance to operate the video camera. Students can predict what will happen using the storyboard on their activity sheets.

4. Have each group illustrate *change over time* by taking a series of four shots:
- first shot—title card;
- second shot—object labelled *before*;
- third shot—object labelled *during*;
- fourth shot—object labelled *after*.

5. Share video with the class.

SOMETHING TO THINK ABOUT

▶ Rather than labelling the three shots with *before*, *during*, or *after*, use a timer beside the object.

Fall Colours

Name _____

1. Colour these leaves:

Summer Leaf

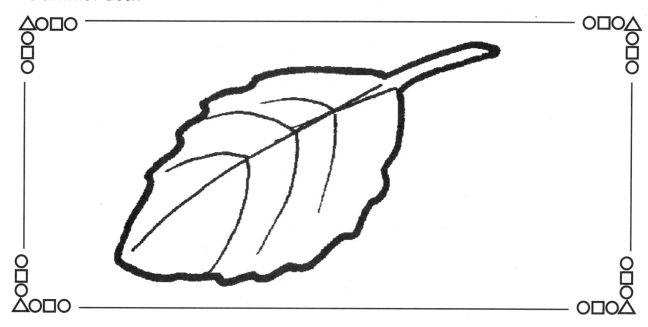

Fall Leaf

Title: **Fall Colours**

Theme: **Environment**

Subject: **Science and Technology**

Materials Needed: Computer, CD-ROM encyclopedia, various green leaves from trees, a blender, rubbing alcohol (water can also be used), white absorbent paper cut in strips, crayons or coloured markers.

Learning Outcomes: • Be aware of recurring events and patterns in their lives.

Inquiry/Thinking Skills: Application, comprehension, and knowledge.

Learning Strategies: Recording.

TEACHING STRATEGIES

1. Explain and discuss with students: "Leaves turn colour in the fall because the leaves stop producing the chlorophyl that keeps the leaves green. The fall colours are there, they are just covered up by the green leaf colour. To see the other colours, you can use chromatography to separate the colours. The molecules of each different colour travel at a different rate and therefore separate when absorbed by the paper."

2. Invite pairs of students to use a CD-ROM encyclopedia to find summer and fall pictures that show foliage. Discuss with them what differences they see between summer and fall leaves.

3. Collect some green leaves and place in a blender with enough rubbing alcohol to make a liquid when blended. Blend the leaves well. Then, place the blended leaves in a clear container so that students can see the contents. Place a strip of absorbent paper so that it just touches the liquid. The paper will absorb the liquid. After a few moments, place the strip of absorbent paper on a piece of white paper to dry. The white paper allows you to see any colour changes more clearly. Challenge students to predict changes to the paper.

4. Ask students to colour a summer and fall leaf on their activity sheets.

SOMETHING TO THINK ABOUT

▶ Try this experiment with other plants.

▶ Separate the colours of black felt markers using paper strips and water. Have students predict what colours they will see.

Four Wheels to Go

Name _____

1. This is how to make a play car.

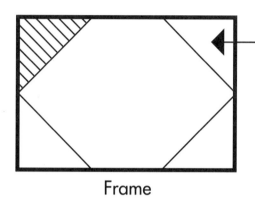

Frame

Glue the 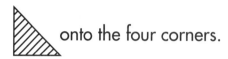 onto the four corners.

2.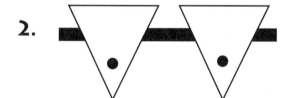

Glue here: two on one side, two on the other side.

Cut out holes.

3.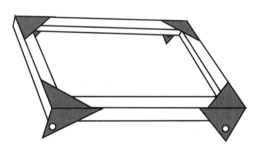

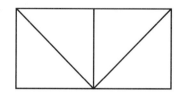

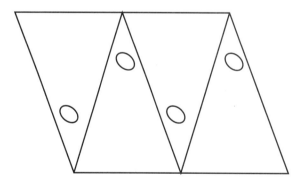

Put axles into holes. Glue wheels onto axles.

4. Now make a top for your car. Go for a ride!

Title: **Four Wheels to Go**

Theme: **Transportation**

Subject: **Science and Technology**

Materials Needed: Square rods for frames, dowel or round rods for axles (or wheels and axles from a building set), cardboard, glue, scissors, paint.

Learning Outcomes:
- Participate actively in a technology activity.
- Demonstrate a knowledge of how to build structures and mechanisms by joining similar materials.
- Safely use tools and materials in building simple structures.

Inquiry/Thinking Skills: Application, comprehension, evaluation, and synthesis.

Learning Strategies: Building a structure, problem-solving, and using a template.

TEACHING STRATEGIES

1. Examine a vehicle that has movable wheels and point out to students how an axle runs between the wheels and is attached to the chassis or *frame*.

2. Trace the triangle templates on their activity sheets or adjust the size on a photocopier depending on how big your students' models will be.

3. Building steps:

a) Glue the triangular pieces onto the corners.

b) Punch a hole near the bottom of the four larger triangles. Glue these pieces to the side of the chassis so that they hang down below the rods.

c) Push the axles through the holes.

d) Glue each of the wheels. For the wheels and axles, you can use parts from a building set or lollipop sticks for the axles and cardboard for the wheels.

4. Encourage creativity in adding detail to the vehicle bodies. Students might glue small boxes to their chassis, then paint windows and doors on them.

5. Encourage students to talk freely when they are evaluating the wheel systems on their vehicles, but insist that they be positive and polite in their comments, especially when commenting on someone else's project.

Fun with Mirrors

Name _____

1. Draw a picture of what you saw in the mirror.

IRWIN
Q
QUICK START MASTERS

Title: **Fun with Mirrors**

Theme: **Experiments**

Subject: **Science and Technology**

Materials Needed: A collection of shiny things, both those provided by teacher and those brought in by students.

Learning Outcomes: • Investigate devices that make use of the properties of light.

Inquiry/Thinking Skills: Application, comprehension, knowledge, and synthesis.

Learning Strategies: Classifying, explaining, observing, and predicting.

TEACHING STRATEGIES

1.   Lay out a collection of objects brought in by students and teacher in which students can see their faces.

2.   Sort the objects by these criteria:
   • very shiny/dull,
   • those in which you can see your face,
   • those in which you cannot see your face.
   Have students draw pictures of the different ways their faces look in the shiny objects. (Their faces will look different.)

3.   Have students take time to play with the mirrors: looking at ceiling designs, at the sky, behind the boiler, and at their name on a card in a mirror; playing "Simon Says" with the mirrors; creating a kaleidoscope, etc.

4.   Ask them to use two mirrors taped together at the edge. Tell them to stand the double mirror up and put an action figure at different angles in front of it. Ask: "What happens?" If they put two mirrors standing facing each other with an action figure in front, ask: "How many action figures do you see?"

5.   Conclude by asking students to draw a picture of what they in the mirror. Encourage them to choose their favourite mirror image.

Gears That Make Patterns

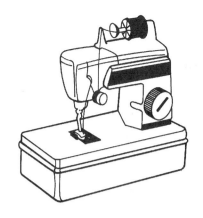

Name _____

1. How big are the gears?

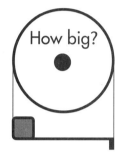

How big?

a) _____

b) _____

c) _____

d) _____

2. What things use gears?

Title:	**Gears That Make Patterns**	
Theme:	**Machines**	
Subject:	**Science and Technology**	

Materials Needed: Samples of gears, spirograph set or a "homemade" gear drawing set, tape measure, various devices that use gears.

Learning Outcomes:
• Ask questions about the world around them and look for answers to these questions, working both alone and with others.
• Listen and speak in order to learn and exchange ideas at work and at play.

Inquiry/Thinking Skills: Analysis, application, and comprehension.

Learning Strategies: Experimenting, explaining, and exploring.

TEACHING STRATEGIES

1. Let students examine various sized gears. Encourage them to describe what they look like (shape, teeth, etc.). Demonstrate that the teeth on the gears can fit together (*mesh*) and turn, even if the gears are of different sizes.

2. Introduce the spirograph set and demonstrate how it works. Invite them to use a spirograph to make patterns using different-sized gears. Before you begin, challenge them to predict what will happen when they use different-sized gears. Ask them to measure each gear they use and record their measurements on their activity sheets and under each pattern.

3. Ask: "Do your patterns repeat themselves? Did it take a long time or a short time for them to repeat? What did you discover about the pattern and the size of the gear?"

4. Discuss with them what machines use gears. Have several of these machines in the classroom for students to examine.

5. Ask them to put a check mark on the machines on their activity sheets that use gears.

Lever Beaver

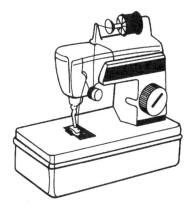

Name _____

1. Attach **A** to **B** with a spread fastener.

2. Attach the other end of **B** to the tail with glue or a staple.

3. Position lever onto back of beaver. Choose the best place for fixed point and attach through lever pieces and the beaver.

4. Tape crosspiece **C** over lower level piece to keep lever in place.

5. Push and pull on lever to make tail "slap!"

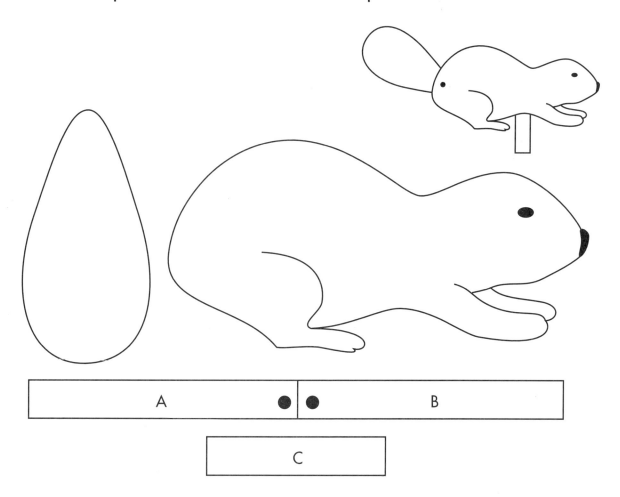

IRWIN
Q
QUICK START MASTERS

Title: **Lever Beaver**

Theme: **Machines**

Subject: **Science and Technology**

Materials Needed: Print and electronic resources about beavers, bristol board, spread fasteners, a building set (optional), the Lever Beaver template (see activity sheet).

Learning Outcomes:
• Identify ways in which pushes and pulls change how something is moved.
• Describe living things and investigate the features that help them survive in their surroundings.
• Demonstrate a knowledge of how to build mechanisms by joining similar material.

Inquiry/Thinking Skills: Application, comprehension, knowledge, and synthesis.

Learning Strategies: Constructing a lever, listening, using a template, and viewing.

TEACHING STRATEGIES

1. Introduce the topic of beavers by reading a story, or viewing a filmstrip or video. Discuss with students the beaver's appearance, food, habitat, and other interesting characteristics. Also talk about how the beaver slaps its tail on the water to warn of danger.

2. Inform students that they are going to make a model of a beaver that will be able to slap its tail. Challenge them to think of ways that they could do this.

3. Present some models of levers—these could be from a building set or cardboard strips strung together with spread fasteners. Introduce the term *lever*. Discuss how levers are sometimes used to make things move (in addition to lifting things). Hold a lever against the blackboard and demonstrate how an end can be moved by holding one of the fasteners at a fixed point and moving the other end up and down.

4. In addition to making a beaver move its tail, discuss other possible applications for the fixed point lever to make an object move (for example, a dog's tail wagging, a person waving, etc.).

5. Have students use the template on their activity sheets to create a beaver with a tail that can "slap." (They can trace the template onto bristol board and cut it out.) Demonstrate how to fasten the lever to the back of the beaver.

   a) Attach A to B with a spread fastener.

   b) Attach the other end of B to the tail with glue or a staple.

   c) Position lever onto back of beaver. Choose the best place for a fixed point and attach through lever pieces and the beaver.

   d) Tape crosspiece C over lower lever piece to keep lever in place.

   e) Push and pull on lever to make tail "slap!"

SOMETHING TO THINK ABOUT

▶ Invite students to put the beaver into its natural habitat by sketching a background on a larger piece of bristol board. They can attach the beaver to the background by gluing around the outside, keeping all moving parts free.

Levers in the Classroom

Name_____

1. What things did you use to get the lid off?

_____

_____

_____

_____

2. Draw small or big levers.

Title:	**Levers in the Classroom**
Theme:	**Machines**
Subject:	**Science and Technology**

Materials Needed: A variety of other classroom objects that operate on the basis of levers (rulers, spoons, screwdrivers, etc.), cans with lids which can be pried off, chart paper, markers, overhead projector, tape recorder.

Learning Outcomes:
- Identify more than one solution to a problem and show respect for other people's solutions.
- Compare the design features of a number of classroom items and indicate which of these features allow people to use these items more effectively.

Inquiry/Thinking Skills: Analysis, application, comprehension, and evaluation.

Learning Strategies: Comparing, concluding, justifying, manipulating, and observing.

TEACHING STRATEGIES

1. Challenge groups of students to open a can whose lid is stuck: "How can you take the lid off?" Encourage students to devise as many different ways as possible using a variety of materials available in the classroom.

2. Have each group demonstrate their procedure. Summarize these ideas on chart paper. Have them look for similarities among these procedures: what materials were used, how materials were used, why the lids came off easier, etc.

3. On chart paper, outline the main principle involving the use of levers: **A lever is a machine that helps us to do things. It uses a bar that will not bend. Sometimes it helps us do things more easily.**

4. Divide students into two groups. One group will look around the classroom for examples of small levers. These will be placed on an overhead projector and projected on the screen for discussion as to function and similarities. The other group will look for larger lever examples that they will identify and explain on an audio tape to be played back as part of their presentation. Ask them to circle on their activity sheets the type of lever they are looking for. Have them write *small* or *big* beside the appropriate lever.

5. With students, summarize what levers can do. Levers can make different kinds of work easier, allow other levers to work, let some things move in different directions, and turn small movements into bigger ones.

6. See also Activity 9, Lever Beaver.

Living and Non-living Things

Name _____

1. Put a circle around what is real.

2. Write a science sentence about living and non-living things.

_____

_____

_____

Title:	**Living and Non-living Things**	
Theme:	**Environment**	
Subject:	**Science and Technology**	

Materials Needed: Computer, primary database or spreadsheet program, potted plant, artificial plant, stuffed animal, live animal (classroom pet).

Learning Outcomes: • Describe living and non-living things and make comparisons among them.

Inquiry/Thinking Skills: Analysis, comprehension, and knowledge.

Learning Strategies: Comparing, describing, and listing.

TEACHING STRATEGIES

1. Observe two kinds of plants: one real, one artificial. Ask pairs of students to use all of their senses to discover the likenesses and differences between the two plants. Repeat with two kinds of animals (real and stuffed). Ask students to put a circle around what is real on their activity sheets.

2. Create a chart on the computer similar to the one below for students to fill in.

Object	Likenesses	Differences
Real Plant		
Artificial Plant		
Real Animal		
Stuffed Animal		

3. Help students to write a science sentence about living and non-living things.

4. Encourage partners to discuss their chart results and share their ideas with the class.

Looking at Sand

Name _____

1. Look at the sand particles. What do you see?

2. How long does it take for the sand to go from **A** to **B**?

A

B

_____

3. Make a sand timer. What things will you need?

_____

_____

_____

Title: **Looking at Sand**

Theme: **Earth**

Subject: **Science and Technology**

Materials Needed:
Hand lenses, tweezers, paper towels or newspaper for covering tables, sand, variety of materials for constructing a sand timer, stopwatch, timer.

Learning Outcomes:
• Describe and demonstrate the use of manipulative materials, tools, and equipment.
• Describe non-living things and make comparisons among them.
• Demonstrate a knowledge of how to build structures and mechanisms by joining similar materials.

Inquiry/Thinking Skills: Analysis, application, evaluation, and synthesis.

Learning Strategies: Comparing, demonstrating, rating, and substituting.

TEACHING STRATEGIES

1. Provide groups of students with some particles of sand to investigate with their hand lenses. Allow for some initial exploration and discussion in their groups.

2. Encourage them to look at individual particles to find out what colours are in a particle and what shape the particle has.

3. Have them sketch on their activity sheets what they see in the sand particles. Their observations could be placed onto a class chart:

Looking at Sand

Sand Grain 1	Sand Grain 2	Sand Grain 3
Sand Grain 4	Sand Grain 5	Sand Grain 6

4. Encourage students to look at their sketches and then to describe how the particles are different and the same.

5. Distribute some small timing devices which have sand in them. Once again allow students an opportunity to explore and investigate their shape, size, function, etc. Have students time how long it takes for the sand to empty from the top to the bottom (from **A** to **B** on their activity sheets).

6. Brainstorm with students how a sand timer could be constructed using the materials available. Challenge them to construct their own sand timers using the materials at hand.

Looking at the Computer Keyboard

Name _____

1. Do you know these keys? Match the little box to the big box.

Shift	moves cursor to the left
Spacebar	hold this down and type a letter to make it a capital
Del	lets you print what's on the screen
Tab	hold this down to type the letter at the top of the key
Esc or Alt	moves the cursor up
↑	lets you move the cursor around the screen
↓	press this to make a space
←···	press this key to make a letter disappear
···→	press this to type in capital letters only
Shift	moves cursor to the right
Clicking on Mouse	press this key to go to the main menu when you want to exit the program
Print Screen	moves the cursor down
CTRL/ALT/DEL	moves cursor to the right five spaces
Caps Lock	lets you reboot the computer

IRWIN
QUICK START
MASTERS

Title: **Looking at the Computer Keyboard**

Theme: **Communication**

Subject: **Science and Technology**

Materials Needed: Computers, scissors, glue, primary word-processing software.

Learning Outcomes:
• Be able to use standard problem-solving techniques in an investigation.
• Compare design features of different computer keyboards as to appearance and function.

Inquiry/Thinking Skills: Application, comprehension, knowledge, and synthesis.

Learning Strategies: Comparing, conducting an investigation, identifying, and matching.

TEACHING STRATEGIES

1. As a class, look at the computer. Identify the components and the correct name for each. Place name cards on the appropriate piece of hardware (monitor, keyboard, CPU-central processing unit, mouse, printer, etc.). Draw students' attention to some of the other keys. Talk about the letters or symbols appearing on these keys. Have students predict what they think might happen when these keys are pushed.

2. Have students cut apart the boxes on their activity sheets. Tell them to match each key (little box) with the description of what happens when it is pressed (big box). Encourage them to talk with their partner about what they think might happen before they try it. Check their matches before they glue them onto a separate paper. (Ensure that gluing is done away from computers!)

3. If possible, show students the keyboard of a different type of computer and discuss similarities and differences. Experiment with various keys to see if they perform the same operations.

Making Colours

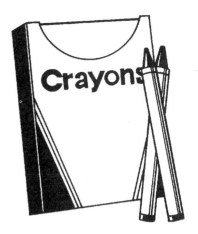

Name _____

1. What colour is the picture?

   a) _____

   b) _____

   c) _____

   d) _____

2. What colours do you see?

Thing	Colour Seen	Real Colour

3. Mixing Colours:

   red   + blue = _____

   yellow + blue = _____

   yellow + red   = _____

4. What colours did you have on your spinner? What new colours did you see?

Title:	**Making Colours**
Theme:	**Colour**
Subject:	**Science and Technology**

Materials Needed: Overhead projector, colour transparencies of primary colours (yellow, red, blue), paints, brushes, paper, icing, food colouring, spinner, knife, baked cupcakes, bowls, flashlight with coloured bulbs, heavyweight bristol board.

Learning Outcomes:
• Ask questions about the world around them and look for answers.
• Use a variety of methods to gather, analyse, display and communicate information.

Inquiry/Thinking Skills: Application, comprehension, evaluation, knowledge, and synthesis.

Learning Strategies: Creating, demonstrate, discovering, observing, and recording.

TEACHING STRATEGIES

1. Have students look at each other with and without sunglasses. Ask: "How do things change? Do you think that things would look different through different colours?"

2. Shine a flashlight on a picture. Next, tape different colours of tissue paper to the flashlight, one at a time. Have students record on their activity sheets what colour the picture becomes.

3. Tell them to pretend they are from another planet and see through red eyes (red overhead transparencies). Place three objects on the overhead projector and have them record once again the colours they see.

4. Ask them to predict how many colours can be made with three primary colours. Mix these colours on the overhead.

5. Make colour spinners: Put a hole in the centre and paint two to three colours with no white spaces on the circle. Push a pencil through the hole and spin on the floor. Ask students: "What happens when the top spins? Red and green give_____; blue and yellow give _____." (See activity sheet.)

6. Give students paints. Have them experiment with other colours.

7. Have students use icing and food colouring to decorate their favourite cupcakes. Say: "Mix two colours for your icing to make a new colour. What colour do you have?"

Making Sound

Name_____

1. Which thing makes sound all by itself?

2. Make a sound harp. You will need:

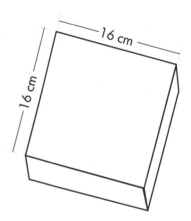

16 cm

16 cm

3. Hammer nails like this. Tie string to nails.

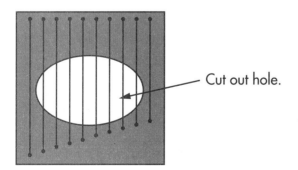

Cut out hole.

4. Play your sound harp.

IRWIN
QUICK START
MASTERS

Title:	**Making Sound**
Theme:	**Experiments**
Subject:	**Science and Technology**

Materials Needed: Various devices that make sound, materials to make a sound harp (see activity sheet), record player, old records, styrofoam cup, paper cone, pin needle.

Learning Outcomes:
• Compare design and features of a number of everyday items and indicate which of these features allow people to use each item most effectively.
• Build a device that produces sound.

Inquiry/Thinking Skills: Analysis, application, comprehension, knowledge, and synthesis.

Learning Strategies: Comparing, constructing, demonstrating, explaining and predicting.

TEACHING STRATEGIES

1. Show students a number of devices that produce sound. Ask them to identify some of these by circling them on their activity sheets. Discuss with students why certain objects do not produce sound. Lead the discussion to a record and record player. Encourage students to understand that a record needs a pick-up device (the needle) and an amplifier (record player or cone attached to needle) to play the sound.

2. Play records on a record player with the sound turned off. Then play the records with various needles made by groups of students. (Put a pin or a tack through the bottom of a styrofoam cup and put some pennies for weights. Roll a cone shape and attach to the end of a pin or needle.)

3. Compare each homemade one to the real record needle. Discuss how it is different and the same.

4. Review with students safety procedures for hammering nails. If this task is too difficult for students, consider having an older student "adviser" for each group.

5. Have groups make a sound harp. (You will need to precut 16 cm x 16 cm or larger wood blocks for each group.) Be sure to have students *tightly* stretch each string. Encourage students to understand that sound travels differently depending on the length of the string. The shorter the length, the higher the sound.

Media Gadgets

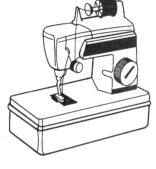

Name _____

Gadget	Parts

Title: **Media Gadgets**

Theme: **Machines**

Subject: **Science and Technology**

Materials Needed: Visual dictionaries, media gadgets.

Learning Outcomes: • Identify characteristics of some media devices.

Inquiry/Thinking Skills: Analysis, comprehension, and knowledge.

Learning Strategies: Comparing, drawing, and sorting.

TEACHING STRATEGIES

1. Brainstorm with students a co-operative list of media devices that we use regularly. Categorize them into large and small devices.

2. Assemble an assortment of small media devices that no longer function. Devices such as remote controls, telephones, radios, watches, clock radios, game controllers, and calculators are usually widely available.

3. Direct students to work in groups to disassemble the devices. Tell them to draw pictures on their activity sheets of two gadgets and some of the parts inside.

4. Ask students to compare similarities in the parts that make up these media gadgets, circling the parts that look the same in both gadgets. They can use a visual dictionary resource to identify some of the parts found inside.

5. Develop a vocabulary list of some of the common elements, such as wires, batteries, transistors, buttons, etc.

Mixing Colours

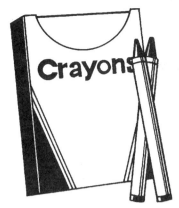

Name _____

1. Light has three primary colours. Can you name them?

    _____

    _____

    _____

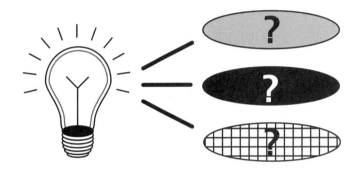

2. Make new colours.

    _____ + _____ = _____

    _____ + _____ = _____

    _____ + _____ = _____

3. What do all the primary colours make?

    _____ + _____ + _____ = _____

Title:	**Mixing Colours**
Theme:	**Colours**
Subject:	**Science and Technology**

Materials Needed: Overhead projector, primary colour acetates (red, green, and blue).

Learning Outcomes:
• Ask questions about colours and look for answers to these questions, working both alone and with others.
• Conduct an investigation and record the results.

Inquiry/Thinking Skills: Application and synthesis.

Learning Strategies: Experimenting, recording, and reporting.

TEACHING STRATEGIES

1. Set up the overhead projector in a convenient place for individuals or pairs of students to work. (Review the handling and safety rules for using the overhead projector.)

2. Provide students with acetate circles in primary colours. Have them use the three coloured circles on the overhead and examine their colours. Explain to them that these colours are the *primary* colours. Ask them: "What are their names?" Have them write the names on their activity sheets.

3. Ask them to experiment by placing two primary colour acetates on top of each other. Demonstrate how to place the acetate on the overhead. Challenge them to write the names of the colours they use and the colour they make on their activity sheets. Tell them these are *secondary* colours. Encourage them to discover what all three primary colours make (white).

4. Discuss with the students the meaning of primary and secondary colours.

SOMETHING TO THINK ABOUT

▶ Experiment with primary and secondary colours using one of the following: paints; food colouring and coffee filters; water-based markers and drops of water; chalk pastels. Remind students that pigment colours (primary: red, yellow, blue) mix differently than light ones.

Oral Observations

Name _____

1.   Draw pictures to show what happened in your experiment.

When we started the experiment:

During the experiment:

When the experiment was finished:

Title: **Oral Observations**

Theme: **Experiments**

Subject: **Science and Technology**

Materials Needed: Tape recorder, tape player, audio tapes.

Learning Outcomes: • Use one method for obtaining and communicating specific information.

Inquiry/Thinking Skills: Application, comprehension, and synthesis.

Learning Strategies: Following directions, listening, recording, and speaking.

TEACHING STRATEGIES

1. Use a tape recorder instead of a print resource for conducting a science experiment that involves observation. Two machines are ideal for this procedure: a playback-only cassette machine (to minimize the possibility of error) and a recorder-player.

2. Instruct students in the operation of the machines. The playback-only machine should be marked as **Player** and be used to play the teacher's prerecorded instructional tape. The Player could be put into the play-pause mode when the activity begins and the pause button clearly marked with a colored dot or tape. The second machine should be marked **Recorder** and used by the students to record their responses. The Recorder should be set in the record-pause mode to minimize operations needed to record. Supply the students with a switching hand microphone if one is available.

3. Set up a simple experiment, for example, comparing things that float or sink. Instead of writing the instructions for students to follow, record them on a cassette recorder. Include an appropriate signal on the tape telling students when to pause to carry out a step (words or a bell).

4. Have students use a second tape recorder to record their observations at each stage of the experiment. When the tapes are played back in sequence, the students can readily review the procedure and the results. Encourage students to record (draw) their experiment on their activity sheets.

SOMETHING TO THINK ABOUT

▶ Some students may create their own tapes of verbal instructions to describe simple procedures such as how to mix paints, pop popcorn in the microwave, etc.

Pulley Magic!

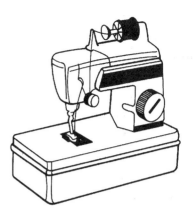

Name _____

1. This is a **pulley**. Find pictures of machines that use pulleys.

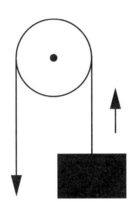

2. Make a pulley machine book.

3. Now make your own pulley machine. See what it can do.

Title Page

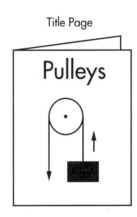

Pulleys

Title: **Pulley Magic!**

Theme: **Machines**

Subject: **Science and Technology**

Materials Needed: String, thread spools, paper clips (for hooks), wire, cardboard boxes, pliers, tape, building set, toy cars or other miniatures.

Learning Outcomes:
- Describe how certain technologies affect their lives and change the environment.
- Investigate phenomena in their immediate environment and beyond and communicate their findings, working both alone and with others.
- Demonstrate an understanding of the operation and function of pulleys.
- Listen and speak in order to learn and exchange ideas at work and at play.

Inquiry/Thinking Skills: Application, comprehension, knowledge, and synthesis.

Learning Strategies: Constructing, explaining, investigating, and viewing.

TEACHING STRATEGIES

1. Arrange for students to observe the custodian raising and/or lowering the flag on the flagpole. Discuss what tools help do this job: rope and wheel at top of flagpole. Identify the wheel as a *pulley*. Talk about the purpose of pulleys: to lift things. Elicit applications: crane, clothesline, tow truck, elevator, climbers in gym, etc.

2. Ask students to search a CD-ROM encyclopedia for pictures of machines that use pulleys. (Students can work in pairs or groups.) Direct them to print out a picture for each pulley machine they find. They can use these pictures to make a pulley booklet (see activity sheet).

3. Challenge students to create a machine that uses a pulley. They might want to construct a crane to lift erasers, a tow truck to pull along a toy car, a small scale flagpole, etc. After the models have been constructed, encourage students to take turns presenting them, explaining how they used the pulleys to do work.

Reduce, Reuse, and Recycle Paper

Name _____

1. Three different uses of paper at school:
    a) _____
    b) _____
    c) _____

2. Here's how we made paper.

Making Our Own Paper Group members: _____ _____ _____ _____	Beginning step:
Middle step:	Last step:

Title: **Reduce, Reuse, and Recycle Paper**

Theme: **Environment**

Subject: **Science and Technology**

Materials Needed: Electric kitchen blender, iron, kettle.

Learning Outcomes:
• Identify and use a familiar technology from the home.
• Identify an environmental issue in the school and experiment with a solution.

Inquiry/Thinking Skills: Application, comprehension, and knowledge.

Learning Strategies: Describing, experimenting, and observing.

TEACHING STRATEGIES

1. This activity may be one of many used to develop students' awareness of our global environment and its protection.

2. Discuss with students what can be done for the environment right inside the school building. Encourage them to see that recycling paper can save trees and landfill space. If there is already a recycling program in place at school, discuss what happens to materials sent for recycling. Otherwise, have the class investigate how to start a recycling program.

3. There are many books and kits that give instructions and procedures for making paper. Choose a recipe appropriate for your class.

4. Collect and organize the materials: *electric kettle*—heating the water; *electric blender*—grinding into pulp; *electric iron*—drying the paper.

5. Review the procedures with students.

6. Have them create a storyboard of the steps using hand-drawn or Polaroid pictures (see activity sheet).

SOMETHING TO THINK ABOUT

▶ Encourage students to use the paper to send a message to others about why it is a good idea to *reduce, reuse, and recycle* paper.

Shadow Fun

Name _____

1. Take three pictures of the puppet play. Or, draw three pictures of the puppet play. Put them on three pages like this:

1

2

3

2. Tell about each picture.

3. What part did you like best?

_____

_____

_____

Title: **Shadow Fun**

Theme: **Light**

Subject: **Science and Technology**

Materials Needed: Projector, screen, paper, pencil shapes on a ruler, Polaroid camera.

Learning Outcomes:
- Describes the results of projecting a variety of objects and shapes using their knowledge of spatial relationships and the effects of motion geometry.
- Investigate and describe simple cause-and-effect relationships.

Inquiry/Thinking Skills: Analysis, comprehension, evaluation, and knowledge.

Learning Strategies: Describing, determining, evaluating, explaining, and observing.

TEACHING STRATEGIES

1. Hang a large white sheet in a darkened place. Behind the sheet, put a filmstrip projector. Ask students to use their hands between the sheet and the projector to experiment with shapes that create animals on the sheet. They can also use black paper to make shapes and attach them to a ruler.

2. Tell students to move their hands back and forth different distances from the light. Ask them: "What happens to the shapes?" (Closer up = *lighter and bigger*; farther way = *darker and smaller.*)

3. Ask: "Where are the darkest parts of the shadow?" (Towards the middle.) "Why?" (The outer edges of the shape are not shaded from the entire light source.)

4. Invite students to sit on the opposite side of the sheet and watch the shadow puppet play. It can be as simple as a conversation between two puppets or it can be a more complex story with several actors.

5. Ask students (or groups) to photograph or draw three interesting parts of the puppet play. Ask them to put these pictures on three pieces of paper (see activity sheet). Encourage them to write something about each picture on the bottom of the page.

6. Challenge students to write (or tell) about the part of the puppet play they like best.

Sound Travel

Name _____

1. What does sound travel in?

a)   b)    c)

d)    e)

2. Make a tin-can phone:

You will need:

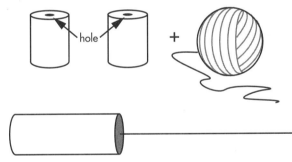

3. What things use sound?

_____

_____

_____

IRWIN
QUICK START MASTERS

Title: **Sound Travel**

Theme: **Experiments**

Subject: **Science and Technology**

Materials Needed: Mediums and materials in which sound travels: balloons, wood, watch, bells, funnel and hose, table, tin-can telephone, rolled funnel of paper, etc.

Learning Outcomes:
• Investigate properties of sound that increase and decrease sound travel.
• Investigate devices that make use of the properties of sound.

Inquiry/Thinking Skills: Comprehension, evaluation, knowledge, and synthesis.

Learning Strategies: Constructing , creating demonstrating, recording, and verifying.

TEACHING STRATEGIES

1. Investigate with students this hypothesis: *Sound travels through all materials and can be heard in a variety of different ways.*

2. Have groups or pairs of students investigate one or more of the following:
• sound travels through string,
• sound travels through air,
• sound travels through water,
• sound travels through wood,
• sound travels through rubber tubing.

Groups can use:
• a tin-can telephone,
• a speaking tube (funnel on each end of rubber hose),
• jangling spoons on the end of a string,
• a ticking watch through a balloon filled with water,
• a dowel rod into a funnel in the ground,
• a ticking watch on one end of a table with an ear on the other end,
• a folded large cardboard cylinder with small end in ear and large end out.

3. Show students how they can make their own tin-can telephone (see activity sheet for diagram).

4. Challenge them to use a CD-ROM encyclopedia to find objects and devices that use sound. Tell them to write the names of three of these devices on their activity sheets.

Sprouting Ideas

Name _____

1. Count out ten seeds.

2. Make your seeds sprout.

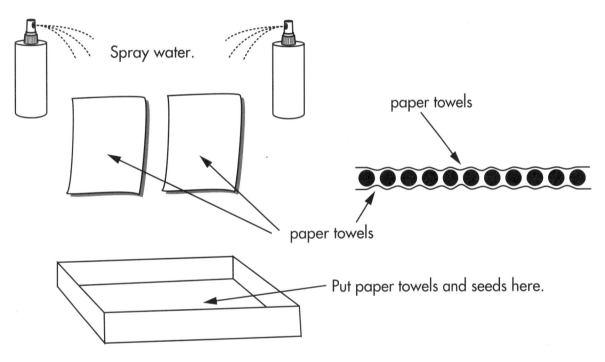

Spray water.

paper towels

paper towels

Put paper towels and seeds here.

3. Rinse your seeds carefully every day.

4. Check to see if your seeds are sprouting.

5. Count how many seeds have sprouted. Tell your teacher this number so that she or he can enter the number into the computer.

Title: **Sprouting Ideas**

Theme: **Plants**

Subject: **Science and Technology**

Materials Needed: Seeds from several different kinds of plants (beans, alfalfa, mung, peas etc.), water, paper towels, containers to sprout seeds, computer, primary graphing software, tape recorder.

Learning Outcomes:
• Use a wide range of processes to gather information and communicate results.

Inquiry/Thinking Skills: Application and analysis.

Learning Strategies: Counting, graphing, and observing.

TEACHING STRATEGIES

1. Discuss with students how the seeds of plants are different and how they can sprout.

2. Give each student or group ten seeds of each plant or have each group work with just one kind of seed.

3. Instruct them to place seeds between wet paper towels and in plastic containers (see activity sheet). If the room is dry, you may need to place a lid on the container to keep seeds from drying out.

4. Have students examine their seeds every day to see if any have sprouted. They should rinse them in cool water each day to prevent mould.

5. As a class, use the computer to graph the results of the sprouting process every day. Discuss why different plants sprout faster; why different sprouts of the same plant sprout differently; why some do not sprout at all.

6. Instead of or in addition to graphing the results, students could explain their results into a tape recorder.

SOMETHING TO THINK ABOUT

▶ Ask students: "What would happen if you cut the seeds first? if you freeze them first? if you try to sprout them in the cold?"

▶ Direct students to plant their seeds, and then measure and graph the rate of growth.

Technology in Our House

Name _____

1. What technology do you use in your house?

2. Who uses the technology in your house?

   ❏ mother   ❏ father   ❏ you   ❏ brothers or sisters   ❏ friends

3. Make a picture dictionary of technology.

C Coffee Maker

What is it used for?
   making coffee

Where is it used?
   kitchen

Who uses it?
   dad, mom

IRWIN
QUICK START
MASTERS

Title: **Technology in Our House**

Theme: **Family**

Subject: **Science and Technology**

Materials Needed: Writing materials, magazines and catalogues, computer, word-processing software, markers, pencil crayons.

Learning Outcomes: • List and define technologies in a picture dictionary.

Inquiry/Thinking Skills: Comprehension and knowledge.

Learning Strategies: Brainstorming and describing.

TEACHING STRATEGIES

1. Brainstorm, as a class or in groups, all the technologies used in the home. Discuss who uses each technology. Create a class chart of the technologies as a vocabulary list for reference.

2. Tell students they are going to make a picture dictionary of technology. Discuss with them the model shown on their activity sheets. (Or, prepare a different example for your students.)

3. Provide magazines and catalogues for pictures of technology devices, or students may draw the pictures. Students may work on a group or individual dictionary. Set expectations of how many pages must be completed before the dictionary is compiled.

4. Invite students to share their completed dictionaries. Encourage them to discuss who has similar technologies at home and who has a technology no one else has.

SOMETHING TO THINK ABOUT

▶ Challenge students to predict what home technologies will be like in the future and what possibilities they might offer people.

Telephone of the Future

Name _____

1. Draw a telephone of the future.

2. Make your telephone.

3. Talk about your telephone.

Title:	**Telephone of the Future**
Theme:	**Communication**
Subject:	**Science and Technology**

Materials Needed: Materials to make a phone: cardboard boxes and tubes, tin cans, string, clear plastic wrap, construction paper, aluminum foil, cardboard, buttons, springs, etc.

Learning Outcomes:
• Compare the design features of several models of telephones.
• Design and build a futuristic telephone (simple structure).
• Describe what has been constructed and how it works.

Inquiry/Thinking Skills: Application, comprehension, and synthesis.

Learning Strategies: Brainstorming, constructing, designing, general problem-solving and reporting.

TEACHING STRATEGIES

1. Make a variety of telephone models available for students to investigate. Compare them in the following ways: shape, size, parts, and special features.

2. Discuss with students how the telephone has changed over time (smaller, more compact, greater number of features, more portable, etc.). Discuss why these would be considered improvements.

3. Challenge students to brainstorm other ways in which phones could still improve: how they could "do things" that they do not or cannot do now. These suggestions could be ideas for the "telephones of the future."

4. Encourage pairs of students to select one of the brainstormed ideas or another one of their own.

5. Ask them to design and construct a phone of the future incorporating this particular feature. Tell them to use their activity sheets to draw their design.

6. Let students use a tape recorder to describe their telephone and its special feature and explain how it works.

SOMETHING TO THINK ABOUT

▶ Students can role-play a year 2050 telephone conversation using their futuristic phones.

Weather Watch—1

Name _____

1. Write your weather words here:

    _____

    _____

    _____

    _____

    _____

2. Here are some tools for looking at the weather. Try to identify them.

    How hot it is   How much rain   How strong the wind is
                           or snow falls

    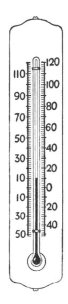   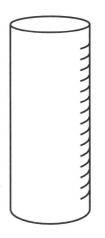   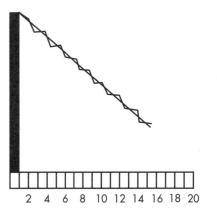

3. Watch a weather show on TV, or hear a weather report on the radio.

Title:	**Weather Watch—1**
Theme:	**Environment**
Subject:	**Science and Technology**

Materials Needed: Weather-related filmstrip and print resources, thermometers, containers for precipitation collection, wind measurement equipment, weather media resources, computer, word-processing software.

Learning Outcomes:
- Ask questions about the world around them and look for answers, working both alone and with others.
- Begin to demonstrate attention to accuracy, thoroughness, persistence, and creativity in conducting an investigation.
- Communicate information orally, using appropriate language and elocution skills.
- Make and read concrete and pictorial simple charts.

Inquiry/Thinking Skills: Analysis, application, comprehension, evaluation, and knowledge.

Learning Strategies: Comparing, constructing, graphing, listening, measuring, recording, and responding.

TEACHING STRATEGIES

1. Show a filmstrip or read a book related to weather (wind, sun, rain, snow, etc., depending upon the time of year). Discuss the various types of weather that we experience and develop a vocabulary list on the blackboard. Have students copy some or all of these weather words onto their activity sheets. Elicit from them how we know what the weather is going to be like. Identify for them some of the tools and devices that are used to measure and predict weather. If possible, display these tools in the classroom.

2. Tell students to listen to a taped weather report and identify what items are included. Discuss how the weather reporters are able to tell about the weather (weather balloons, measuring equipment, etc.). Three simple devices are shown on their activity sheets.

3. Introduce the idea that they are going to be junior weather reporters for the school. Brainstorm what tools and equipment they will need to report on the weather. Challenge them to identify the weather tools on their activity sheets.

4. Help students write a weather report using some or all of their weather words. If they are comfortable working with words, encourage them to write on the computer. Others might draw a weather picture and then write their weather words on the illustration.

Strategies continued in Activity 27, Weather Watch—2.

Weather Watch—2

Name _____

1.   Weather Facts

Day of Week	☀️🌥️🌧️	Rain or Snow	Wind

2.   Weather News

Today is _____.

It is _____ (sunny, partly cloudy, cloudy, rainy).

_____ cm of _____ (rain or snow) **fell yesterday.**

It is _____ (not windy, windy, very windy) **today.**

3.   Record your weather news on tape.

Title: **Weather Watch—2**

Theme: **Environment**

Subject: **Science and Technology**

Materials Needed: See Activity 26, Weather Watch—1.

Learning Outcomes: See Activity 26, Weather Watch—1.

Inquiry/Thinking Skills: See Activity 26, Weather Watch—1.

Learning Strategies: See Activity 26, Weather Watch—1.

TEACHING STRATEGIES

1. Tell students they are going to collect and/or create the tools and equipment they will need to be a junior weather reporter: a container with measurements on it to gather precipitation, a thermometer, a tool that will help measure how strong the wind is and from what direction it is blowing. (See activity sheet of Weather Watch—1.)

2. Decide on the best size and shape of container to measure rain or snow accumulations. Have students put a measurement scale on the side. Provide opportunities to read a thermometer. Discuss ways to measure direction and intensity of the wind. The wind tool might be as simple as a piece of cloth attached to a ruler or the students could create a windsock that is attached to the school building. Some discussion of wind direction might be necessary, too. Decide on a wind rating scale, for example: no wind, light wind, strong wind, very strong wind, wind gusts.

3. Discuss ways of recording and sharing their information with the others in the school. Ask students to keep track of the weather for one school week. (See activity sheet for organizer.)

4. Introduce the idea that sometimes the weather reporters on the radio, television or in the newspaper are not accurate in their predictions. Discuss possible reasons for this. Let students take turns listening to media weather reports and recording this information. Encourage them to make comparisons and analyse their findings. Discuss why there might be differences in the measurements (drifting snow, temperature taken in windy area, broken thermometer, etc.).

5. Encourage pairs or groups of students to complete the Weather News report on their activity sheets. Tell them to choose the appropriate word in brackets. Encourage them to read their report to a partner.

Winter Dens

Name _____

1. Some bears hibernate in dens during the winter.
What does **hibernate** mean?

   _____

2. Which bears hibernate in the winter?

   _____

3. Where do bears hibernate?

   _____

4. Make your own bear den. Here are some things you can use:

   stones   dry grass   leaves   twigs   branches

5. Give a name to your shoe-box home.

Title: **Winter Dens**

Theme: **Bears**

Subject: **Science and Technology**

Materials Needed:
CD-ROM encyclopedia; shoe box; variety of natural materials (stones, twigs, leaves, dried grass, etc.); variety of classroom materials, such as paper, plasticene, pencils, markers.

Learning Outcomes:
• Investigate attributes of two- and three-dimensional figures by constructing a model.
• Demonstrate knowledge of how to build a structure.

Inquiry/Thinking Skills: Analysis, comprehension, and synthesis.

Learning Strategies: Constructing and research.

TEACHING STRATEGIES

1. Discuss with students what *hibernate* means. Ask them if they know of any animals that hibernate. Remind them that many bears in northern climates hibernate. Tell them: "Some bears hibernate during the winter months. These bears hibernate in their own special kind of place."

2. Invite students to use a CD-ROM encyclopedia to find out about bears. Ask them to answer the questions on their activity sheets. Encourage them to draw pictures to help in their answers.

3. Challenge students to design and build a shoe-box bear's den. Encourage them to use classroom materials and, if possible, some of the natural materials pictured on their activity sheets. Encourage them to make a plasticene bear model for their den.

SOMETHING TO THINK ABOUT

▶ Discuss with students why some animals hibernate in winter (food is scarce in winter, travel is difficult in heavy snow, etc.).

▶ Ask them if winter makes people want to hibernate, too.